Internet Marketing Dictionary

Written by

Tim Beachum
Chris Beachum

The Internet Marketing Dictionary was something that we gave to our clients as a gift. It was meant to be a token of our appreciation and to help the clients understand what we were talking about. We understood that most clients are busy focusing on the day-to-day activities of their business and did not have time to keep up with the new terms that popup online on a daily basis.

Lets face it, we live in the digital age, and the internet in one way or another has become a part of our daily lives. It would best serve you if you understood the lingo that was surrounding you.

As always if you have any questions our would like to contact Tim or Chris please give us a call at -757-271-5605

Visit us online:
http://www.4thgc.com

Other Books by
Tim and Chris Beachum

Marketing for Local Business Owners

301 Redirect – A 301 redirect automatically causes one url to redirect to another and tells the Web (and search engines) that this redirect is permanent, as opposed to a temporary (302) redirect. 301 redirects are generally preferable for Search Engine Optimization purposes and are therefore often referred to as search engine friendly redirects.

404 Server Code – The 404 or Not Found error message is a standard response code indicating that the client was able to communicate with a given server, but the server could not find what was requested.

Above the Fold – The part of the page you can see without scrolling down or over. The exact amount of space will vary by viewer because of screen settings. You often pay a premium for advertisement placements above the fold, which will add to the costs of internet marketing services, but may also add to results.

adCenter – Microsoft adCenter powers paid search results on Microsoft's bing, Yahoo! (as of November 2010), and other sites within its network. Microsoft adCenter is now the second largest paid search provider in the United States.

Advertising Network – A group of websites where one advertiser controls all or a portion of the ads for all sites. A common example is the Google Search Network, which includes AOL, Amazon, Ask.com (formerly Ask Jeeves), and thousands of other sites. In Google AdWords, they offer two types of ad networks on the internet: search and display (which used to be called their content network).

AdWords – AdWords is Google's paid search marketing program, the largest such program in the world and in most countries with notable exceptions such as China (Baidu) and Russia (Yandex). Introduced in 2001, AdWords was the first pay per click provider offering the concept of Quality Score, factoring search relevancy (via click-through rate) in along with bid to determine ad position.

Affiliate Marketing – A type of internet marketing in which you partner with other websites, individuals, or companies to send traffic to your site. You will typically pay on a Cost per Acquisition (CPA) or Cost per Click (CPC) basis.

Algorithm – The term search engines use for the formulae they use to determine the rankings of your Natural Listings. Search engines will periodically send a spider/bot through your website to view all its information. Their programs (bots) analyze your sites data to value your site and fix whether or not, and how high or low pages on your site will appear on various searches. These algorithms can be very complicated (Google alone currently uses 106 different variables) and search engines closely guard their algorithms as trade secrets.

ALT Tags – HTML tags used to describe website graphics by displaying a block of text when moused-over. Search engines are generally unable to view graphics or distinguish text that might be contained within them, and the implementation of an ALT tag enables search engines to categorize that graphic. There is also talk that business websites will all be required to utilize ALT tags for all pictures to comply with certain American Disability Act requirements.

Analytics– Also known as Web Metrics. Analytics refers to a collection of data about a website and its users. Analytics programs typically give performance data on clicks, time, pages viewed, website paths, and a variety of other information. The proper use of Web analytics allows website owners to improve their visitor experience, which often leads to higher ROI for profit-based sites.

Anchor Text – The clickable words of a hypertext link; they will appear as the underlined blue part in standard Web design. In the preceding sentence, "hypertext link" is the anchor text. As with anything in SEO, it can be overdone, but generally speaking, using your important keywords in the anchor text is highly desirable.

Astroturfing – The process of creating fake grassroots campaigns. Astroturfing is often used specifically regarding review sites like Google Places, Yelp, Judy's Book and more. These fake reviews can be positive reviews for your own company or slander against your competitors. Not a good idea, and could lead to your IP being blacklisted. The worse case scenario is a lawsuit.

Backlinks – Links from other websites pointing to any particular page on your site. Search engines use backlinks to judge a site's credibility; if a site links to you, the reasoning goes, it is in effect vouching for your authority on a particular subject. Therefore, Link Building is an incredibly important part of Search Engine Optimization. How many links, the quality of the sites linking to you, and how they link to you all are important factors. Also called Inbound Links.

Baidu – Serving primarily China, Baidu is the largest non-US based search engine in the world (although it was started in the United States). Sites can be optimized for Baidu and they offer their own paid search service.

Banned – When pages are removed from a search engine's index specifically because the search engine has deemed them to be violating their guidelines. Although procedures are starting to loosen up somewhat, typically a search engine will not confirm to you that your site has been banned or why it has been banned. If you knowingly did something against the rules (written or unwritten) that got your site banned, you can probably clean up your act and get back in the game. We hear stories that, from time to time of companies hiring Search Engine Optimization companies that deliver great, fast results, leave town, and then their website mysteriously disappears from the rankings. Google won't tell them why their site got banned, so the company ends up left out in the cold unless another company can come in and backwards engineer the issues, unravel the work, and get the search engine to reinclude the site.

Banners – Picture advertisements placed on websites. Such advertising is often a staple of internet marketing branding campaigns. Depending upon their size and shape, banner ads may also be referred to as buttons, inlines, leaderboards, skyscrapers, or other terms. When using specifics, banner ads refer to a 468×60 pixel size. Banner ads can be static pictures, animated, or interactive. Banner ads appear anywhere on a site – top, middle, bottom, or side. Banner costs vary by website and advertiser; two of the most popular pay structures are Cost per 1,000

Impressions (CPM) and flat costs for a specified period of time.

Behavioral Targeting (BT) – An area of internet marketing becoming increasingly refined, behavioral targeting looks to put ads in front of people who should be more receptive to the particular message given past Web behavior, including purchases and websites visited. The use of cookies enables online behavioral targeting.

Bing – Bing is Microsoft's search engine, which replaced live.com in June 2009. Bing results now power Yahoo!'s search for paid (except display; through Microsoft adCenter) and organic (except local listings) through an alliance entered into between the two Web giants in December 2009. The deal cleared regulatory concerns in early 2010 and was fully completed in November of the same year.

Black Hat SEO – The opposite of White Hat SEO, these Search Engine Optimization, or SEO, tactics are (attempted) ways of tricking the Search Engines to get better rankings for a website. If not immediately, using black hat methods will eventually get your site drastically lower rankings or banned from the search engines altogether. While there are completely legal and ethical techniques you can use to improve rankings, if you design and market a website mostly for humans and not for the search engines' you should be okay.

Blog – Short for Web log, blogs are part journal, part website. Typically the newest entry (blog post) appears at the top of the page with older entries coming after in reverse chronological order. Several blogging platforms exist; our favorite is WordPress.

Brand Stacking – Multiple page one listings from a single domain. Prior to 2010, a site would be fortunate if it had three first page results for branded searches. Since Google tweaked its algorithm to include Brand Stacking, that number has risen to as many as eight of the top search rankings.

Categories – Words or phrases used to organize blog posts and other pieces of information, such as albums for photos. Categories are generally broader than tags and used in instances when there will generally be multiple posts or other data points per category.

ccTLD – ccTLD's are "Country-code" TLD's showing what country a site is focused on or based in. Using Google and the United Kingdom as an example, Google UK is google.co.uk. Sometimes these ccTLD's are two sets of letters separated by a period (e.g. "co.uk" for the UK or "com.au" for

Australia) and sometimes they are just one set of letters (e.g. ".fr" for France).

Use of separate websites on unique ccTLD's is typically viewed as the best way for exporters to target other countries via search engine optimization. However, site owners can also target outside countries through other means such as through country-focused subdomains or even subdirectories.

Click through Rate (CTR) – # of clicks / # of impressions. Click through rate is a common internet marketing measurement tool for ad effectiveness. This rate tells you how many times people are actually clicking on your ad out of the number of times your ad is shown. Low click through rates can be caused by a number of factors, including copy, placement, and relevance.

Cloaking – Showing a search engine spider or bot one version of a Web page and a different version to the end user. Several search engines have explicit rules against unapproved cloaking. Those violating these guidelines may find their pages penalized or banned from a search engine's index. As for approved cloaking, this generally only happens with search engines that offer a paid inclusion program. Anyone offering cloaking services should be able to demonstrate explicit approval from a search engine for what it is they intend to do.

Content Management System – Content Management Systems (CMS) allow website owners to make text and picture changes to their websites without specialized programming knowledge of software like Adobe Dreamweaver or Microsoft FrontPage. Content Management Systems can be edited by anyone with basic word knowledge via an internet connection. No need for length or costly web development contracts or need to wait on someone outside your company to make changes. CMS examples include WordPress, Drupal, and Joomla.

Content Network – Each major search engine offers a form of content network within its paid search interface, typically referred to as content networks, although Google just renamed their content network the Google Display Network. Within Google AdWords, advertisers have two options for content network advertising:

1. Pick sites. With this option, you can choose the actual sites, or in some cases, sections and pages of sites, on which you want to display your ads.

2. Contextual advertising. Contextual advertising allows you to use keywords like you would in traditional paid search advertising and the search engines will display your ads next to articles,

blog posts, and other Web pages that are related to those keywords.

Both options are great for inexpensive brand awareness on massive scales in addition to more direct means such as lead generation. The days of buying remnant display ads not being worth it are behind us.

Content Tags – HTML tags which define the essence of the content contained within them and readable by search spiders. These include Header and Alt Tags.

Contextual Advertising – A feature offered by major search engine advertisers allowing your advertisement to be placed next to related news articles and on other Web pages. Contextual advertising seeks to match Web content from the display page with your advertised search term(s). Contextual advertising isn't perfect (what in life is?), but it's come a long way from its inception to the point where it can provide great value to advertisers when used correctly.

Conversion Rate – This statistic, or metric, tells you what percentage of people is converting (really!). The definition of "conversion" depends upon your goals and measurements. It could mean a sign up for free information, a completed survey, a purchase made, or other.

Cookie – Think of cookies like Batman's Bat Tracer. When you visit a website, Batman sticks a cookie on your browser to follow you around. Batman can then go back to his Bat Cave and watch where you're going and where you've been. A little Big Brother-ish to be sure, but cookies also provide direct benefits to surfers, including remembering passwords and bringing you offers in which you are genuinely interested (see Behavioral Targeting above).

Cost per Acquisition (CPA) – An online advertising cost structure where you pay per an agreed upon actionable event, such as a lead, registration, or sale.

Cost per Click (CPC) – A common way to pay for search engine and other types of online advertising, CPC means you pay a pre-determined amount each time someone clicks on your advertisement to visit your site. You usually set a top amount you are willing to pay per click for each search term, and the amount you pay will be equal or less to that amount, depending on the particular search engine and your competitors' bids. Also referred to as Pay Per Click (PPC) or Paid Search Marketing.

Cost per Impression (CPM) – A common internet marketing cost structure, especially for banner advertising. You agree to pay a set cost for every 1,000 Impressions your ad receives. Search engine marketing may involve CPM costs for Contextual Advertising. This internet advertising pay structure should really be called Cost per 1,000 Impressions.

Crawler – Component of a search engine that gathers listings by automatically "crawling" the Web. A search engine's crawler (also known as a Spider or robot) follows links to Web Pages. It makes copies of those pages and stores them in a search engine's index.

CSS – CSS – short for Cascading Style Sheet – is a way to move style elements off individual Web pages and sites to allow for faster loading pages, smaller file sizes, and other benefits for visitors, search engines, and designers.

Customer Relationship Management (CRM) – Software solutions that help enterprise businesses manage customer relationships in an organized way. An example of a CRM would be a database containing detailed customer information that management and salespeople can reference in order to match customer needs with products, inform customers of service requirements, etc.

Day Parting – Day parting refers to serving ads at different times of the day and days of the week, or even changing bids or copy / creative at different times. For example, you may not want your ads to show from 11AM-2PM on Tuesdays. This can be done manually in most online platforms, or automatically in some such as Google AdWords. Automated day parting is not currently available directly through many social media advertising platforms such as facebook ads and LinkedIn direct ads.

Delisting – When pages or whole websites are removed from a search engine's index. This may happen because, but not necessarily, they have been Banned.

Description Tags – HTML tags which provide a brief description of your site that search engines can understand. Description tags should contain the main keywords of the page it is describing in a short summary – don't go crazy here with Keyword Stuffing.

Directories – A type of search engine where listings are gathered through human efforts rather than Web crawling. In directories, websites are often reviewed, summarized to a brief description and placed in a relevant category.

Domain Name – A website's main address. 4th Generation Communication's domain is www. 4thgc.com.

Doorway Page – A Web page created to rank well in a search engine's organic listings (non-paid) and delivers very little information to those viewing it. Instead, visitors will often only see a brief call to action (i.e., "Click Here to Enter"), or they may be automatically propelled past the doorway page. With cloaking, they may never see the doorway page at all. Several search engines have guidelines against doorway pages, though they are more commonly allowed through paid inclusion programs. Also referred to as bridge pages, gateway pages and jump pages and not to be confused with Landing Pages.

Domain Name Monitoring – Watching Domains across various extensions. Some companies offer to do this for, say a .com site by checking the same domain name in .net, .org, .eu, etc.

eCommerce – The ability to purchase online. eCommerce also goes by other super-snazzy names like etail. website features that allow ecommerce are commonly called shopping carts.

EdgeRank – The algorithm facebook uses to rank a page's or profile's posts to determine which of those posts will appear in the newsfeeds of users connected to those pages and profiles (or pages and profiles tagged in the posts). The higher an EdgeRank, the more likely you will appear in the newsfeeds. Facebook does not release this data publicly, neither for the pages, nor individual posts.

Ego Keyword – A keyword an individual or organization feels it must rank for in either or both natural listings or paid search results regardless of cost and Return on Investment. Read more about ego keywords.

Email Campaign System – Email is perhaps the most overlooked and underutilized (based on cost and effectiveness) form of internet marketing today. Email campaign systems allow organizations to send out emails to their email lists with a standard look and feel. Features often include the ability to segment lists.

Enhanced Bidding – A feature specific to Google AdWords. When you select to utilize enhanced bidding, you're giving AdWords the power to adjust your bidding in order to increase conversions. With this feature, you can pay up to 30% over the keyword bid that you set. Think of it like a hybrid between CPC and CPA bidding, albeit still more heavily weighted toward cost per click. Be careful with enhanced bidding – many search engine marketers will tell you that they have had poor experiences with cost per acquisition bidding within AdWords.

Eyetracking – A process that allows testing of websites for usability or any other purpose. Eyetracking is performed by a small number of companies utilizing high speed cameras to monitor and record where the eyes of test subjects actually move on screen.

Facebook Retargeting – While this term can also refer to other forms of retargeting, it is most often used to mean serving ads to prior site visitors while those visitors are on facebook. Facebook opened its ad exchange in December 2012 to allow partners to offer facebook retargeting.

Feed – Coming in an XML language that uses either RSS or Atom formatting are an extremely popular way for organizations to get their messages through the clutter and into the hands of interested parties. With the simple click of an orange button (right), users can stay connected to a site's content (Blogs, news, podcasts, etc.) automatically anytime their computers are connected to the internet. That button will connect you to the feed for the Found Blog.

Forum – A place on the internet where people with common interests or backgrounds come together to find information and discuss topics.

Geo-Targeting – The ability to reach potential clients by their physical location. The major search engines now all offer the ability to geo-target searches in their Pay-Per-Click campaigns by viewing their ip addresses. Geo-targeting allows advertisers to specify which markets they do and don't want to reach.

Golden Triangle - Eye-tracking studies show an "F" shaped pattern that most people tend to look at most often when looking at Search Engine Results Pages. These patterns vary slightly among the different Search Engines, but show the importance of placement among Natural Listings and Pay-per-Click ads.

Google AdWords Certified Partner – Google AdWords offers the most extensive certification process of any of the paid search marketing providers. The Google AdWords Certified Partner program replaces the earlier Qualified Google Advertising Company / Individual program.

Graphical Search Inventory – Banners and other types of advertising units which can be synchronized to search keywords. Includes pop-ups browser toolbars and rich media.

Header (or Heading) Tags () – HTML heading and subheading tags are critical components of search engine marketing, as often times both are graphical, thereby unreadable to search engine spiders. Optimally, page titles should also be included to clearly define the page's purpose and theme. All of the header tags should be used according to their relevance, with more prominent titles utilizing <h1>, subheaders using <h2>, and so on.

HTML– HyperText Markup Language, the programming language used in websites. Developers use other languages that can be read and understood by HTML to expand what they can do on the Web.

Hyperlink – Often blue and underlined, hyperlinks, commonly called "links" for short, allow you to navigate to other pages on the Web with a simple click of your mouse.

Image Maps – Clickable regions on images that make links more visually appealing and websites more interesting. Image maps enable spiders to "read" this material.

Impressions – The number of times someone views a page displaying your ad. Note that this is not the same as actually seeing your ad, making placement and an understanding of the site's traffic particularly important when paying on a Cost per 1,000 Impressions basis.

Inbound or Incoming Links – See Backlinks

Index – The collection of information a search engine has that searchers can query against. With crawler-based search engines, the index is typically copies of all the Web pages they have found from crawling the Web. With human-powered directories, the index contains the summaries of all the websites that have been categorized.

Internet Marketing – Any of a number of ways to reach internet users, including Search Engine Marketing, Search Engine Optimization, and Banner advertising. Direct Online Marketing™ specializes in these internet marketing services.

Internal Linking – Placing hyperlinks on a page to other pages within the same site. This helps users find more information, improve site interaction, and enhances your SEO efforts.

Interstitial – An ad that appears between two pages a person is trying to view. The ad often appears near a hyperlink allowing someone to quit viewing your ad and go directly to the page he or she originally tried to access. Direct Online Marketing™ typically does not employ this type of advertisement as part of its internet marketing services.

JavaScript – JavaScript – not to be confused with its distant cousin Java – is an Object Oriented Programming language developed by NetScape. It is used primarily to improve user experiences on websites with enhanced functionality.

Keyword – Almost interchangeable with Search Term, keywords are words or a group of words that a person may search for in a Search Engine. Keywords also refer to the terms you bid on through search engine marketing in trying to attract visitors to your website or Landing Page. Part of successful Search Engine Optimization is including keywords in your website copy and Meta Tags.

Keyword Stuffing – When the Web was young and search engines were starting to gain in popularity, some smart website owners realized that the search engine Algorithms really liked some Meta Tags. Really liked them. So they started stuffing a bunch of keywords, often with high search volumes and no relevancy to the site, into title, description, and keyword tags. Sites instantly rocketed to great SERPs. Soon thereafter the search engines changed their ranking formulae and the sites lost their positions or were outright Banned.

Key Performance Indicator (KPI) – a particularly important performance measurement. A business may use KPIs to evaluate its success, or to evaluate the success of a particular activity in which it is engaged.

Keyword Tags – HTML tags which define the keywords used on Web pages. Meta keyword tags used to carry great weight with some older search engines until they caught up with the spammers using this practice and modified their algorithms. Today Google is officially on record for not giving these tags any weight.

Landing Page – The first page a person sees when coming to your website from an advertisement. This page can be any page on your website including your home page. Almost anytime you direct someone to your website from an advertisement, you should send them to a specialized landing page with tailored information to increase your landing page conversion rate. Radio advertisements are a notable exception as spelling out specific URL's can be time consuming and difficult to remember. Direct Online Marketing™ has extensive experience in creating, testing, and modifying landing page conversion rates to give your business the highest quality, least expensive, most cost effective leads possible.

Link Building – The process of obtaining hyperlinks (links) from websites back to yours. Link building is a crucial part of Search Engine Optimization.

Link Popularity – How many websites link to yours, how popular those linking sites are, and how much their content relates to yours. Link popularity is an important part of Search Engine Optimization, which also values the sites that you link out to.

Local Search – A huge and growing portion of the search engine marketing industry. Local search allows users to find businesses and websites within a specific (local) geographic range. This includes local search features on search engines and online yellow page sites. Optimizing for local search requires different practices than for traditional Search Engine Optimization.

Local Business Listings – Each of the major search engines offer local business listings that appear next to maps at the top of the page on many locally targeted searches. Business may either submit new requests or claim existing local business listings if the search engines have already added the company to the results. Having a website is not required for having a local business listing.

Long Tail Keywords – Rather than targeting the most common keywords in your industry, you can focus on more niche terms that are usually longer phrases but are also easier and quicker to rank for in the search engines. Long tail keywords can amount for up to 60% or so of a site's search traffic.

Meta Search Engine – A search engine that gets listings from two or more other search engines rather than crawling the Web itself.

Meta Tags (see also keyword tags, description tags etc.) – Meta tags allow you to highlight important Keywords related to your site in a way that matters to Search Engines, but that your website visitors typically do not see. Meta tags have risen and fallen in terms of valuation by internet marketers and search engines alike (see Keyword Stuffing), but they still play an important role in Search Engine Optimization. Examples of meta tags include Header Tags and Alt Tags.

Microblogging – Microblogging refers to platforms allowing you to post information in snippets of 140 characters at a time via phone or Web. Twitter quickly became the dominant global player to the point where its name is synonymous with microblogging. In China, however, there are other popular microblogging services, generically called weibo.

Mobile Marketing – As cell phone technology advances, advertisers can not reach their target audience virtually anywhere. While mobile marketing is really just an extension of online marketing, it provides businesses many new opportunities and challenges.

Natural Listings – Also referred to as "organic results", the non-advertised listings in Search Engines. Some search engines may charge a fee to be included in their natural listings, although most are free. How high or low your website is ranked depends on many factors, two of the most important being content relevance and Link Popularity.

Naver – Naver is Korea's largest search engine and Web property. They offer paid search programs, although their pay per click program for non-Korean marketers has primarily been offered through Yahoo! / Overture – Korea. Naver's closest Korean competitor is Daum.

Opt-in – This type of registration requires a person submitting information to specifically request he or she be contacted or added to a list. Opt-ins typically lower lead flow rates and raise Costs per Acquisition from internet marketing campaigns, but may produce higher percentages of interested leads.

Opt-out – Here people are automatically signed up to receive contact, but can opt out of receiving newsletters, calls, etc. at any time.

Organic Listings –See Natural Listings.

Outbound Links – Links on any Web page leading to another Web page, whether they are within the same site or another website.

PageRank – PageRank is a value that Google assigns for pages and websites that it indexes, based on all the factors in its algorithm. Google does release an external PageRank scoring pages from 1-10 that you can check for any website, but this external number is not the same as the internal PageRank Google uses to determine search engine results. All independent search engines have their own version of PageRank. Potentially interesting fact: PageRank was named for Google's Larry Page and it is calculated at the page level – pun fun!

Paid Inclusion – Advertising program where pages are guaranteed to be included in a search engine's index in exchange for payment, though no guarantee of ranking well is typically given. For example, Looksmart is a directory that lists pages and sites, not based on position but based on relevance. Marketers pay to be included in the directory, on a CPC basis or a per-URL fee basis, with no guarantee of specific placement.

Paid Listings – Listings that search engines sell to advertisers, usually through paid placement or paid inclusion programs. In contrast, organic (natural) listings are not sold.

Paid Placement – See Paid Search below.

Paid Search – Also referred to as Paid Placement, Pay Per Click, and sometimes Search Engine Marketing, paid search marketing allows advertisers to pay to be listed within the Search Engine Results Pages for specific keywords or phrases. Paid placement listings can be purchased from a portal or a search network. Search networks are often set up in an auction environment where keywords and phrases are often associated with a cost-per-click (CPC) fee. Google AdWords and Yahoo! Search Marketing are the largest networks, but Microsoft adCenter (live.com) and other sites also sell paid placement listings directly as well.

A good search engine marketing company offering Paid Search will select an exhaustive set of industry-related Search Terms, set up your accounts, write advertising copy, create Landing Pages, control your bidding (how much you're willing to pay per Search Term click) and budgeting, and test and refine your advertising for effectiveness.

Pay-for-Performance – Term popularized by search engines as a synonym for pay-per-click, stressing to advertisers that they are only paying for ads that 'perform' in terms of delivering traffic, as opposed to CPM-based ads, which cost money, even if they don't generate a click.

Pay per Click (PPC) – See Cost per Click (CPC), above. The most common type of search engine advertising cost structure is PPC search engine marketing. Google, Yahoo, MSN, and many more search engines all use PPC.

Permission Marketing – Along the lines of Opt-in registrations, permission marketing focuses on receiving the consent of users before being contacted or, in some cases, even seeing an advertisement. Permission marketing is centered around the concept that people are increasingly tuning out the barrage of advertisements they see each day. Its focal tenet is that a business will have a better chance of gaining a client when the client first gives permission to be sent an ad or contacted. Search engine marketing by its nature can be thought of as a type of permission marketing – showing advertisements to people already searching for that information – as long as the ad is relevant to what they are searching.

Pop-Under – An advertisement that opens in a new Web Browser window once you visit a particular page or take some other action. Considered less annoying than Pop-Up ads because the new window appears behind the existing one.

Pop-Up – An extremely abused type of online marketing advertisement, pop-ups open new windows on your screen that partially or wholly cover your current Web Browser window. Some search engines ban ads that create a certain number (or even any) pop-up ads. Direct Online Marketing™ does not include pop-ups or pop-unders as part of its internet marketing services.

Press Optimization – The optimizing of press releases for search engines. This process has many similarities to Search Engine Optimization, although it focuses much more on Keyword use in content creation in regards to how press releases are often picked up by Blogs and other forms of new media.

Query – Query is another term for "keyword" or "search term." Within Google AdWords, search query reports show the actual terms that searchers used to click on your ads, as opposed to the advertised keyword that is in your account. These two sets of words may or may not be the same.

Rank – How well a particular Web page or website is listed in the Search Engine's Results. For example, a Web page about apples may be listed in response to a query for "apples."

However, "rank" indicates where exactly it was listed – be it on the first page of results, the second page or perhaps the 200th page. Alternatively, it might also be said to be ranked first among all the results, or 12th, or 111th. Overall, saying a page is "listed" only means that it can be found within a search engine in response to a query, not that it necessarily ranks well for that query. Also known as position.

Real Simple Syndication (RSS) – An increasingly popular new technology that allows information to be easily shared on websites or given directly to users per their request.

Reciprocal Link – A link exchange between two sites. Both sites will display a link to the other site somewhere on their pages. This type of link is generally much less desirable than a one-way inbound link.

Remarketing – Remarketing is Google AdWords's term for retargeting.

Results Page – Also referred to as a Search Engine Results Page.

Retargeting – Think of retargeting like cyberstalking. Someone performs an action (often a visit to your site) and has a cookie placed on her or his browser. Then as they go visiting other sites around the Web, your ad appears in front of them, as a banner or other type of display ad, on whatever sites they visit – so long as that site accepts ads from the ad network you use for retargeting. Retargeting can be done through various ad networks and platforms.

Return on Investment (ROI) – The key statistic for many companies: are your advertisements generating profits, and how much profit given the money you have had to pay. Direct Online Marketing™ always has its eye on ROI for all partners…and you should, too!

Rich Media – Web advertisements or pages that are more animated and/or interactive than static Banners or pages.

Robot or Bot – See Crawler.

Robots.txt – A file used to keep Web pages from being indexed or to tell which pages you want a search engine to index.

Run of Site (ROS) – A contract specifying Run of Site means that a Banner or other type of online advertisement can appear on any page, and usually in any open placement, of a particular website.

Scraping – The process of copying content from one Web property and using it on another. In other words, stealing. Scraping technologies have evolved because of the needs for content and to stay ahead of legitimate content creators trying to protect what they've written. Some companies offer content monitoring to help protect against scraping.

Search Engines – Search engines are places people go to search for things on the internet, such as Yahoo!, Google, or bing. Most search engines provide websites two ways of appearing: Natural (free) and Paid. Natural Listings, also referred to as organic listings, appear based on the search engines' own formulae. You can't pay to have your site listed higher (although some search engines require that you pay to be included in the Natural listings), but you can perform Search Engine Optimization (SEO). Paid Listings usually appear above or to the side of Natural listings and are typically identifiable as advertisements. The most common cost for advertising on Paid listings through Paid Search is Pay per Click (PPC).

Search Engine Marketing – All forms of marketing involving search engines – chiefly Search Engine Optimization and Paid Search Marketing. Sometimes this term will also be used to refer to Paid Search exclusively.

Search Engine Optimization (SEO) – A fancy way of saying "making your site search engine friendly". Search engine optimization is typically difficult to do on your own, especially given the increasing complexity and differences among all the search engines. Two important factors that rank highly in all major search engines are Link Popularity (how many websites – and how highly ranked those sites are – link to you) and relevant content (how pertinent information on your website or a particular Web page is to a search).

Search Engine Reputation Management (SERM) – Think of Search Engine Reputation Management as online spin control. SERM allows a person or organization better positioning through strategy involving Search Engine Optimization, Paid Search Marketing, Press Optimization, Blogging, and Social Media. The most important part of SERM is starting early – before a crisis.

Search Engine Results Page – Search Engine Results Pages, or SERPs, are the Web pages displayed by any Search Engine for any given search. They display both Natural (organic) Listings and Pay-Per-Click ads. How high you are listed and where your ad is shown depends on Search Engine Optimization; and paid Search Engine Marketing respectively.

Search Retargeting – A specific type of Retargeting that allows an advertiser to show ads to searchers of given keywords who have never visited the advertiser's site.

Search Terms – A search term is a word or group of words that a person types into a Search Engine to find what they are looking for. Based upon what a company sells, a website should incorporate the most popular or most popular specific search terms into the copy as Keywords. Figuring out the appropriate search terms to put into a website and to advertise on is a huge part of a Search Engine Marketer's job.

SEM – Acronym for search engine marketing and may also be used to refer to a person or company that does Search Engine Marketing – either Paid Search, Search Engine Optimization, or both.

SEO – Acronym for Search Engine Optimization and may also be used to refer to a person or company that does search engine optimization.

Site Retargeting – The most common form of retargeting: displaying your ads to a visitor based on a visit to your site, or individual page of your site. These cookie-based can appear on any publisher throughout the ad network being used. Various targeting options exist, including only showing ads when a certain page has been visited (such as a landing page) and an action has not been completed (e.g. a conversion).

Social Commerce - Selling goods directly online through through social media channels. Just like "electronic commerce" was shortened to "ecommerce", social commerce is sometimes shortened to "s-commerce" or "f-commerce," the latter short for "facebook commerce."

Social Media - A type of online media where information is uploaded primarily through user submission. Web surfers are no longer simply consumers of content, but active content publishers. Many different forms of social media exist including more established formats like Forum and Blogs, and newer formats like Wikis, podcasts, Social Networking, image and video sharing, and virtual reality.

Social Networking – A type of Social Media, Social networking websites allow users to interact and create or change content on the site. These sites, of which businesses are now using for marketing purposes, allow users to create their own websites / online spheres (e.g. LinkedIn and facebook), share photographs (e.g. flickr), microblog / text small bits of information to their personal community (e.g. twitter) or recommend information for others to find on the Internet (e.g. del.icio.us and Digg). The sites in this last grouping are also referred to as social bookmarking or social news sites. There are also a growing number of sites that are heavily dependent on mobile and geographic locations, such as foursquare.

Spam – Can refer to unwanted data sent via email or put on a website to game a search engine. You're probably aware of spam in the classic email sense and hopefully also aware of the strict standards and penalties associated with the CAN-SPAM Act. Spam to a search engine is Web content that the search engine deems to be detrimental to its efforts to deliver relevant, quality search results. Some search engines have written guidelines about what they consider to be spamming, but ultimately any activity a search engine deems harmful may be considered spam, whether or not there are published guidelines against. Examples of spam include the creation of nonsensical doorway pages designed to pleased search engine algorithms rather than human visitors, or heavy repetition of search terms within a page (i.e., the search terms are used tens or hundreds of times in a row). Spam derives its name from a popular Monty Python skit.

Spider – A noun and a verb, Search Engines have spiders crawl through all the linked pages of a website to gather information to include the site in their Natural Listings and also use to determine their ranking on various Search Terms.

Stickiness – How often people return to a website. Constant updates, news feeds, and exclusive content are all ways to make a site stickier.

Submission – The act of submitting a URL for inclusion into a search engine's index. Unless done through paid inclusion, submission generally does not guarantee listing. In addition, submission does not help with rank improvement on crawler-based search engines unless search engine optimization efforts have been undertaken. Submission can be done manually (i.e., you can fill out an online form and submit) or automated, where a software program or online service may process the forms behind the scenes.

Tags – Words or phrases used to describe and categorize individual blog posts, videos, and pictures. Correctly using tags organizes content for users and can help with visibility through SEO and social media optimization.

Targeting – Shaping internet marketing campaigns to attract certain specific groups of prospective clients. Examples of Targeting include women, gun owners, and Medicare recipients. Behavioral Targeting is a newer, specific type of focus for advertisers.

Text Ad – An online advertisement that contains only written copy. Paid listings found on the results pages of the main Search Engines are currently Text Ads, although this is starting to change. Soon you should expect to see video ads pop up here occasionally.

TLD – TLD stands for Top Level Domain. The TLD is determined by whatever comes at the end of a domain name at its root – meaning without any page names.

Tracking Code – Information typically included in the URL that allows an advertiser to track the effectiveness of various aspects of an advertisement. Commonly tracked items include Search Term and referring Search Engine. 4th Generation Communications™ relies heavily on tracking code because tracking results is the only way to determine how effective our internet marketing services are.

Twitter Retargeting – Serving ads to people who have visited your site (or performed some other action) as promoted tweets or promoted accounts while they are on twitter. These ads go across devices, so you can reach visitors on mobile as well as desktop. Twitter is currently offering this type of advertising in beta only through a few select ad network partners.

URL – Uniform Resource Locator. These are the letters and symbols that make up the address of specific Web pages.

Unique Value Proposition (UVP) – In essence, what it is that sets your product, service, or company apart from others and why potential clients should care enough to choose you.

Universal Search – The placement of multiple types of results within a general search so that a user receives images, videos, local search results, news articles, and more next to general Web pages. Also called blended search.

Usability – How easy it is for a user to navigate a website and find the information he or she is seeking.

Viral Marketing – A newer method of internet marketing that attempts to make advertisements so interesting that viewers will pass them along to others free of charge to the advertisers.

Web 2.0 – A trendy buzzword for the internet marketing services industry, but also a legitimate idea and movement: the internet as a platform. Wikis, MySpace, and user-edited search all operate under this premise.

Web Browser – The program you use to access the internet. Common browsers include Microsoft Internet Explorer (IE), Apple's Safari, and Mozilla Firefox.

Webinar – "Web Seminar". These virtual seminars allow people from anywhere in the world to attend via an internet connection. They offer tremendous opportunities for businesses to reach out to people over large geographic areas at low costs.
Web Metrics – See Analytics.

Weibo – Weibo refers to microblogging in the Chinese market. Unlike the rest of the world where twitter is the only major player at this point, China has two major competing weibo services: Sina Weibo (#1) and Tencent Weibo (#2). A key advantage of these weibo platforms over twitter is the amount of information individual Mandarin characters can convey. Therefore, a single weibo post (tweet) of 140 characters can convey as much information as two paragraphs in English and other languages.

White Hat SEO – Used to describe certain Search Engine Optimization (SEO) methods, being "white hat" means using only SEO techniques that are completely above board and accepted by the Search Engines. Doing the opposite (Black Hat) can lead to your website seeing its rankings drop drastically – or being banned altogether – even if the search engine optimization tactics aren't currently banned by search engines.

Wiki – A user-written, -controlled, and –edited site. Anyone with web access can change information appearing on Wikis, which can be about broad or specific topics. Wikis are becoming increasingly popular websites as people search for quality and (hopefully) unbiased information.

WordPress – WordPress is an extremely popular Content Management System. Developed originally for blogs, WordPress offers a great degree of flexibility and functionality.

XML – Extensible Markup Language. Content developers use this language with a variety of forms of content, including text, audio, and visual in order to allow users to define their own elements and pull the data at their pace. XML has played a huge part in the transformation of the Web towards Web 2.0.

Yandex – Yandex is the fastest growing search engine in the world, serving primarily Russia and other countries formerly part of the Soviet Union. It has been experimenting with an English-based search engine, but its main operations are for its Cyrillic engine. They do also offer a Google AdWords-like paid search program.

Z-Index – Using the z-index property of CSS allows you to better control positioning of overlapping elements. This element is sometimes used for black hat SEO purposes.

www.ingramcontent.com/pod-product-compliance
Lightning Source LLC
Chambersburg PA
CBHW051257170526
45165CB00004B/1749